G000094915

The Little Blue Book

A girl's guide to owning your professional development.

Dedication

This book is dedicated to you.

You, who want to jumpstart your professional development, but are at a loss as to where to start. Whether you are just out of college or several years into your career, this is for you.

It doesn't matter what your gender, ethnicity, background or future goal is. ALL OF US go through similar challenges, and I wrote this to show you a path that worked for me.

Throughout these pages, I will share with you a path that will help you stop relying on luck to drive your career, and instead become more intentional about your professional goals.

Contents

Introduction

You have been in your job for some time now, with steady execution and no major areas of attention in your performance reviews, but you feel stuck. It is hard to explain, but you have a feeling that it is time to do something more. Maybe it began with the feeling that there is something missing, a feeling of emptiness, or just plain boredom. The best way to describe it is a desire to change something that, although unclear, needs immediate attention. Later, as time passes, that burning desire starts bubbling until it grows and becomes a need to take some sort of action. Take advantage of that moment, because there is no better time. Start too early, and it will be too unstructured and result in a lot of wasted energy. Wait too long and the exhilaration of a new task at hand will fade, leaving you back at square one, but this time disappointed because you know you could have done more.

You might ask yourself: Where do I turn? What should I change? What do I want to do next?
How do I know if it is the right thing to pursue and not another nonsense idea?

Well, you will not know that for sure, but I will tell you that if you do not do something about it, it will drive you crazy, so you might as well take the time to figure it out. You have to start by defining your intent. All fruitful activities in your personal and professional life should start with intent on your part. To do this, you need to dig into the deeper areas of yourself and discover your hidden passions. Your own career path is in your hands, this is the perfect time to make it happen, and we are going to kick it off together.

And then the excuses and limiting beliefs start to bubble up: I am a minority, I am woman in a male-dominated environment, I work with a lot of nasty people, I want

_____ role but can't do that because I have small kids, I am a single mother, and so on. Pardon my bluntness, but you have to get rid of the excuses. As valid as your "reasons" may be, you are your own obstacle. FYI, I am a woman, a mom, and a minority, and for over 20 years I have maneuvered through many male-dominated environments. I do check a bunch of boxes, but it is my strong belief that we all have a choice. We can choose to be a victim of the circumstances that surround us or use those circumstances to toughen up and jump to the next step on the staircase. That is the key! It is a staircase and not an elevator. You must create small goals that, while allowing you to celebrate small victories, also provide you with the strength to continue your journey.

Let's start with a few short steps to get us off on the right foot:

Step 1: Get rid of the what-ifs

There is nothing that kills creativity faster than thinking of all the potential failure scenarios. Although it is helpful to be prepared, it is also important to clear your mind of negative thoughts; after all, this is your life we are talking about. You must realize that your fears and limitations most often come from a fear of failure, sprinkled with the insecurities created by what success looks like for others. You must realize that what works for others might not work for you and vice-versa. Like any other project, think about the true risks you face and find alternatives, but be careful of falling into the never-ending cycle of analysis paralysis. I guarantee you that most of the time you are overthinking a nonexistent risk.

Step 2: Get out a pen and paper

No serious business proposal or credible business has ever succeeded through just talking about it. You can imagine it, envision it, and affirm it, but you also must plan it. Think about it: Would you accept a business proposal with no plan supporting it? How about a contractor coming to your house and verbally describing the work that will be done? Would you pay right away? Like any serious project, we are going to strategize, plan and execute with firm intentions. We will thoroughly prepare in order to succeed and make the most of your strengths, needs, and wants. We are going to be as thorough as possible but also understand that it will never be perfect. Think about it as a contract with yourself. We will define the approach and take it to a point where we feel we can start executing and evolve from that point on. As a consultant once told me: "It is never ever done. We just run out of time."

Step 3: Get serious

In order to make this happen for you, you must dedicate yourself to it. There can be no substantial success with half effort or with the thought of "we will get to it when we get to it". You must set a firm deadline for yourself. Your self-improvement plan must be completed by a certain date, and for that to happen, you will need to break down the work into achievable small steps.

You will need discipline to dedicate the proper amount of time and effort to make it a reality. Set aside time for yourself, preferably the same time every week, so that you learn to expect it and can prepare to be completely focused. Maybe on Sunday morning before everyone wakes up or reserve a conference room during lunch. Make time for you and only you. The question is: Are you ready to make a serious commitment to yourself? I sure am ready to kick this off with you.

"The purpose in life is not to be happy. It is to be useful, to be honorable, to be compassionate, to have it make some difference that you have lived and lived well."

-RALPH WALDO EMERSON

Chapter 1: Find Your North

I picked my degree out of practicality. I knew engineering might be the way to go, given that I was problem-solving practically since birth, but I needed a degree that would be versatile enough to guarantee consistent employment and allow me to pay my student loans. You see, when you are part of a fragile economy, you are always frantically on the watch for the few scarce job opportunities. Then once you are employed, you are petrified for the possibility of being laid off. So that is how I picked industrial engineering, a degree with deep roots in operating systems that you can apply to practically any industry you can think of. I also sprinkled in electrical and computer engineering course work, which allowed me to learn how to code and wire PLCs, and control panels, just in case. (I do have to say that the last course work has come incredibly in handy with Christmas lights.)

Once I had my first job, my fear never truly subsided, although I now realize I had nothing to worry about. You see, my brother and I inherited my father's stubbornness (more on that later), his inability to be complacent, and his sick work ethic. The last two characteristics are an asset for any employer but are not that good for our physical, emotional, and spiritual health.

We were taught to work and to work very hard to achieve. Achieve what? I was never sure, but I needed to achieeeeeveeee. Work while sick, work while disappointed, work while exhausted, work, work, work. My performance reviews have been always the same: Achieves above expectations, exceeds expectations, or my latest one significantly exceeds expectations. I had one boss tell me, "You would rather make yourself sick than fail at work." I took it as a compliment, but I should have taken it as a warning sign.

In summary, I've always been the perfect combination desired by any employer. Work myself to the bone and living in fear of losing my job.

Looking back, I never truly stopped to think about what motivated me. In addition, I was never exposed to someone completely fulfilled with their career, thus I never knew that was a possibility. Do not get me wrong; I do not have any regrets. It was my "normal" and I never really stopped to think about alternatives. The problem with this lifestyle is that although you do achieve and you get the big projects, the big promotions, and the fancy titles, you also burn out quickly. One day, while dragging your feet to work, you stop achieving and you can't pinpoint what exactly happened to you.

Was I successful? You may see it that way. After all, I had a fat salary, the fancy car, and the super long title. All those things are considered signs of success in our society. But was I happy and fulfilled? Nope!

I did not recognize it as burnout at that point, but I was conscious of the symptoms and remember asking myself many times, "What is wrong with me?". A few of the signs I can remember:

- I had always been an early bird; now I could not wake up on time.
- I hated swiping my access card through the office building entry reader. I hated that beep sound followed by the green "you are in" light. I so badly wanted it to be red.
- Tasks that used to take me 15 minutes would now take me an hour to complete, leading to many late nights.
- Overindulging in foods that do not fuel your body to perform. (No judgment here, I have just always preferred a somewhat balanced approach to food).
- Consistent stomach issues.
- Consistently exhausted, even if I had just woken up.
- Consistently in an irritable mood.
- Completely disengaged.

I remember thinking that maybe if I got a new project, that it would encourage me, never mind the other gazillion things I had on my plate. I remember thinking maybe I should talk to someone, but I did not want to be a burden to anyone else. I loved being self-sufficient and that was not going to change any time soon. How naïve...

I should have gotten myself a mentor. I should have had a sense of my personal motivators and my passions. I should have continued to explore several paths under the guidance of my purpose. I should have... But then I would not have had the inspiration to write this book for you, would I?

So... YOU ARE WELCOME for going through so many stumbles so that I can be of service to you!

These days, while either mentoring or coaching, I always start with two questions: What does success mean to you? Why would that vision of your success make you happy? I also share the importance of three core ideas: thinking creatively about professional paths, creating an end goal, and developing a basic plan to get there. Start thinking about these by conducting a self-assessment. This is incredibly important because it will become your guiding light. Basically, what I am asking is for you to understand where you are going because until you define your destination, any vehicle you climb in to and any road you take will seem great.

All your journeys in life should start by understanding you. What makes you happy? What motivates you? What makes you shine? What energizes you? And most importantly, what are your values?

Let's imagine that we do not have any limitations. Imagine for a moment that you have all the skills, financial resources, etc. This is difficult, especially as you face a blank sheet of paper and I am not hiding that fact. But assuming unlimited resources, what would you want your life to be like? What is north on your compass?

It is very important to understand your north, as throughout your career and life there will be many pivot points. Sometime, something that looks great may not be actually a good choice. At times, it may even feel like every road ahead jeopardizes your values. Having a basic understanding of your ultimate vision and supporting core values will help you establish your non-negotiables.

What would you like to be remembered for? How would you like people to feel about you? How would you like to feel about yourself? When you think of your dream, what do you see?

All these questions are key to framing your passions, purpose, and ultimately your path. In the business world, this translates to the vision/mission of the company. What will you do? Who do you want to do it for? How you will do it? Although your purpose (vision and mission) should be revisited and updated periodically, the essence should stay the same. For example, if your purpose is to be a resource to enhance other people's lives, when you revisit in a few months, it probably will not be to make others miserable. Another important note is that being rich and making tons of money is not a purpose. It may be a result of pursuing your passions when directed by your purpose, but it is not the purpose.

Don't have a purpose, or can't think of a passion? No worries. Think about what energizes you, what makes you happy, and what fulfills you. One of my favorite books on this topic is Mastin Kipp's *Claim Your Power*. He walks you through a journey of the happiest and most meaningful moments of your life, which ultimately results in the identification of your purpose and in this way enables you to live a powerful life.

Another approach is through a bit of professional introspection.

Let's go through your career and overall professional experience. Use your resume as a guide, especially if you have been in the workforce for a while. Let's assume that you've had some exposure to other teams, maybe through projects, volunteer work, previous jobs, etc. Throughout your experiences, you've probably had assignments, special requests, and/or other opportunities that exhilarated you, while some others made you wish you could have paid someone to invent a time travel machine to get it over with. Now, if most of your work falls into the time travel machine bucket, we have another problem and this exercise will not be helpful for you. But let's assume that we have some balance of some sort. Think about those experiences in detail. I mean a lot of detail. Think about who made the request: What does he/she look like? How did that request make you feel? Was the request aligned with your skill set? Did you have to work by yourself or with others? How did the teammates involved in that new request make you feel? Was it an easy request or a challenging one? What was the easiest part? What was the most challenging part? How long did you think it would take you to complete? How long did it actually take? How did you feel after it was completed? What was the ultimate result of that?

As an example, I will use my own case.

During a very intense time in my company, my boss's boss asked me if I could be a coach for the upcoming intern class that summer. To be honest, I was annoyed. I remember thinking: Wasn't anyone else available for that? Why did I get stuck with more work?

Then I started to ask questions (outside my brain this time):

Me: How many interns?
Boss's boss: Six.
Me: What will the interns do once they are here?
Boss's boss: They will be assigned to several departments.

18

Me: Do they have specific projects? What does the current intern program look like?

Boss's boss: There is an undergraduate development program, but the focus on identifying the best candidates (recruiting). There is not that much in place once they are in.

Me: ...

Boss's boss: ....So?

Me: So, you are really asking me to build an intern program before the interns come, which leaves me with almost two months to do that and use the upcoming interns as guinea pigs. Did I get that right?

Boss's boss: I knew you could do it!

Me: Sigh...

And that is how my company's intern program started. Guess what? I had a lot of fun doing it. I used my skill set of program design and delivery in a new context, which allowed me to test the transferability of my skills. I enlisted key peers to represent their departments. Together, we came up with killer projects that challenged the interns and also helped each of our departments. Then we pulled a senior leader from each department to serve as a mentor for an intern in another department. At the end of the program, we documented everything we did, tweaked a few elements to generalize some of the specifics, and used that program as a staple for future intern classes. The following year, I gave that program to another person while I served as an advisor. I had a blast, but aside from that, it helped me identify a few areas where I could personally develop and a lot of others where I could serve as a resource. It also helped me determine which skills were transferable and the departments where those skills could be applied. In a nutshell, it helped me identify my next career move.

Back to you. Let's start with the common and feared list of pros and cons. Sorry, but that list is the beginning of many things, and as we mentioned, we must get out a pen and paper and make this a reality. As I shared before, use your resume as guidance. If you are in your first role out of school, think about your course work during high school or college. There is always a lot to uncover because, sometimes without realizing, we are often exposed to multiple roles.

I need you to think about your previous jobs and think about the details of those jobs. I am going to give you a couple of questions to get started, and you can write the answers in that notebook of yours:

- What was your favorite job? Why?
- What was your favorite part of that job?
- What made it so great?
- Within the same job, what things were just okay to do?
- What things did you like the least?
- What was your most hated job?
- Why did you hate it so much?
- What was the most draining part of that job?
- Did you ever get a special assignment? What was that?
- Was there anything good about any assignment?
- What was the good part of it?
- Did it feel refreshing or did you hate the time spent on it?
- What were some of your accomplishments?
- What happened afterward?

Go ahead, think...and write!

Now that you have thought a little about your journey, let's narrow down what you like and what you don't like.

Let's also think about your strengths and your weaknesses, which might be what you are good at or not good at, but I like to think more about what produces an exhilarating experience versus what emotionally drains you. Because you will naturally be drawn to the exhilarating part and will want to do more of that, thus eventually becoming good at it if you are currently not. Now, it is important to highlight that not all the exhilarating experiences will make you happy all the time. There will be tough challenges, but the difference is that these challenges should be temporary. It is important that you develop strong resilience in the process of achieving your goal. Gay Hendricks on the Big Leap refers to this beautifully. Coming from Florida, he wanted to learn how to ski. The first few times he tried it, he felt like a tractor had run over him, but he was determined to really enjoy skiing, so he went for it many times until he got the hang of it.

It is hard to talk about resilience when everything you do seems so hard. Personally, I think resilience is completely connected to the capacity of living a life with purpose. Go back to your vision and core values, which for me personally now guide 95% of my decision making. When you are trying to decide whether to push through or let it go, the decision should also be influenced by your ultimate destination and purpose, without jeopardizing the elements that define you. It also should go back to how bad you want it, and if you are willing to go through several iterations to achieve it, no matter how miserable the process may feel. There is a huge difference between a temporary defeat and a miserable existence.

For me, success is 50% showing up, 25% trusting yourself and the value you know you can provide, and the remaining 25% is resilience and not giving up. The next step? **Stay curious and elevate!**

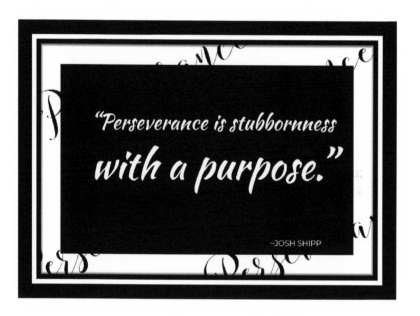

"*Perseverance is stubbornness with a purpose.*"

~JOSH SHIPP

Chapter 2: Stay Curious and Elevate

I think that if I were to look at my life from 25,000 feet above me, I would see that I have been pretty consistent being inconsistent. Do not get me wrong; I am a very structured person, a planner by nature whose life revolves around checklists. However, I have applied these standard traits in to as many environments as I could get my hands on, and I have tried as many things as possible. If there is a project that requires temporary help, I raise my hand. If they are looking for someone to mentor a new employee, I raise my hand. If someone needs assistance during a transitional period, you know the drill. This has provided me insight into different areas than the one that I work in, allowing me to see firsthand a day in the life. Sometimes it becomes a few months in the life, but you get the idea.

You must be careful with this strategy because if the new tasks do not align with your ultimate purpose, main goals, and overall happiness, you can burn out quickly. However, if you are thoughtful about how you approach this, you can have a wealth of knowledge in a very short time period. Two items of caution: 1. Make sure that when you commit to something extra, you truly have the capacity to do it, and 2. Make sure that you can establish strong boundaries.

I remember a period in my career where I was volunteering so much that when I stopped raising my hand because I was over capacity, I was then "voluntold". At first, I was flattered, but over time I realized that it was easy for my manager to just assign whatever was needed to me. After all, I had already volunteered for all the other assignments, and they were always completed on time and under budget. When that happens, you get rewarded with more work. That led to resentment on my part. The key is to take a step back, assess where you are and where are you heading, and evaluate your situation from a few points of views. This challenge can be an opportunity to initiate a wonderful conversation about your career. In my case at the time, the overload of work became a problem because I was too shy to speak up for myself, I needed job security, and I felt super lucky to have the opportunity to work for such a big company.

I have always been resourceful and a problem solver, so it turned out okay, but it took a toll on me physically and emotionally. It seemed like forever, with many months of feeling like I was drowning until I gathered the courage to raise my hand, this time to halt the overload of work. At that point in time, my solution was to quit, but looking back on it, that was not a smart move.

I have made many decisions based on strong emotions, typically fear, but needless to say, this does not always yield the best outcome. The problem with not doing a fair self-assessment of the cause and effect of your decisions leading to the current situation is that you are going to repeat that pattern in your new endeavor. These days, I use my emotions as my compass. If I am fearful, I force myself to go back to the drawing board, dissect the effects of my current situation, and pause to evaluate the true essence of the challenge.

After a series of not-so-smart decisions, I forced myself to do a self-assessment. If I am going to thrive, I need the following:

1. I need to feel that I am always learning something
2. I need to feel challenged and supported
3. I need to feel that what I do supports a larger vision and that the larger vision is in alignment with my personal purpose

If I do not have these elements, I function in robotic mode until I overwhelm myself enough to transition to survival mode. Now, it is important to note that I do not expect that all these things will be given to me, because they will not, but I can work on crafting an environment that enables me to function with the above three precepts.

It took me a lot of bruises and scars to get that understanding, but it made my life so much easier. Let me show you.

Let's say that you have a job and you feel amazing about it. It is the best job you've ever had in your life or the best job you could have ever hoped for. Will it be 100% perfect?

Absolutely not! But can you make it perfect for you? Yes! This is how I did it.

First, I needed to understand myself better, and that includes working every day on getting over myself. I DO NOT need to know everything. Also, it is okay to make a fool of myself from time to time. The embarrassment shall pass, and if it doesn't, it will not hurt anything but my ego. I've gotten to understand that my ego has been very helpful in keeping me safe from harm, but it is not the best decision tool. I have also gotten to understand that with failure comes knowledge. The way I see it is that with so many failed experiences, technically the list of unknowns should be getting shorter. I am going to make a dumb mistake, and that is okay. Even the greatest minds out there had a "dumb moment" or a moment they weren't proud of.

With the above clear and settled within me, I create my own development plan.

There is a fantastic book that was recommended to me by my sister-in-law called *The First 90 Days* by Michael D. Watkins. In that book, I found great perspective on creating a plan for my own success. I re-read it from time to time to make sure I am fresh on the approach to my own growth strategies.

For my development plan, I use three pillars: My current job, my career aspirations, and my personal goals.

My Current Job:
I carefully study my job description. It is very important to keep track of the requirements and expectations for the listed responsibilities. To that, you can add the additional "stuff" that is part of your job now.

My exercise looks like this:

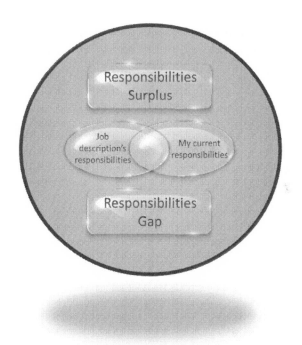

Next, I ask myself:
- What is the reason for the gaps?
  - Are they applicable to my job still? (obsolete, transferred to another role, etc.)
  - Am I equipped to do them?
  - Do I need to learn anything else to do my job?

- What is the reason for the surplus tasks?
    - Are they necessary for my job, or necessary for my ultimate goal or purpose?
    - Are they necessary for my job and need to be added to my job description?
    - Was I asked to do them, or did I volunteer to do them?

Next to that, I list the skills that I have mastered and the skills that I am still trying to develop. I also highlight the surplus tasks that are neither necessary for my job, nor my purpose. Eliminating these types of tasks from my plate will provide the time to develop key skills that I need to move forward.

My Career Aspirations:
While it is important to have a grasp on your current role, it is also very important to be aware that you will not only grow into your role but given enough time, you will also grow **out** of it. This means that once you feel you have a grasp on your responsibilities, you should start thinking about your next steps.

For me, it goes like this:

- Based on my purpose and core values (as described in the Finding My North chapter), is there any role that looks interesting, appealing, and that aligns with my purpose?
- What does the job description look like?
- Do I know anyone who has done that role effectively?
- Did you research the role? No? Do a lot of research. Yes? Do a bunch more.
- What skills do I need to fulfill that role effectively?
- What skills do I need to gain?
- Does it seem like I am overqualified? If so, would that be the right move, or would it be a steppingstone to a better role?

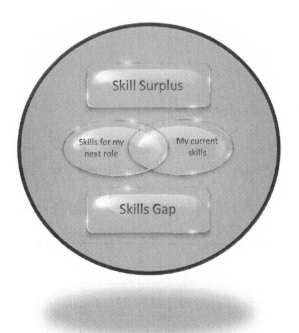

Now I should have two sets of gaps that provide areas to develop. The first one is the set of gaps for my current role and the second one is the set of gaps for my desired role. Almost there.

My Personal Goals:

You are clear on your professional path, but you are more than your job. You are a person with desires and dreams, and that needs to come into the equation. So back to purpose assessment (as described in the Finding My North chapter):

- What makes me happy?
- How I would like to be remembered?
- What fulfills me?
- What is my zone of genius?
- What activities I can do or what service I can provide that helps me achieve this?
- What activities I am doing today that consume my time but do not contribute to my professional or personal growth?

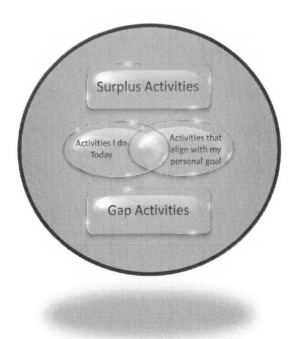

Third time's the charm!

Now combine the three lists of gaps and consider the activities and involvements that you have on your plate today. Compare and contrast to identify similarities and synergies between current and/or long-term goals. How about a quadrant to portray the results?

Let go of the non-value-added activities, look for alternatives in which you are involved but not consumed, and alternatives that serve a double purpose. You can do that in any of the following ways:

a. By delegating ("Here is a professional development opportunity for you Dave!")
b. By excusing yourself if it is voluntary work (maybe instead you could serve on the board, which will help you professionally as well)
c. By talking to your manager and seeing what you can swap

As far as the gaps in your skill set, explore potential opportunities to close them. For this, feel free to think as creatively as you want, as the sky is the limit. Is there a new special project that you can volunteer for? Can you shadow someone? Can you have a cup of coffee with someone who is really good at the skill you are trying to master? Is there a professional association you can join?

You can also start by educating yourself on the areas where you have gaps through books, podcasts, and training.

Now that you have a solid understanding of your gap closure plan, share it with your manager and ASK FOR FEEDBACK!

Believe me, a good manager should be happy to see that you are taking ownership of your career. You do have to be careful here because some leaders are just not that good at providing feedback, but even if this is the case, I recommend that you look at the essence of the feedback and avoid being bogged down by the method in which the feedback was provided. For example, you can take out any conflicting element in the messaging and focus on the message being provided. Does this message apply to me? Is it a question of differences in working styles or is it a valid observation?

Follow up periodically to make sure your manager is aware of your current workload and your progress towards your goal.

Below is a sample agenda for your one-on-ones:

- Recap of actions from previous discussion and status
- Current priorities
- What is working and what is not
  - Solutions you have thought about
- Career goals and your plan to get there
- New opportunities for growth

- ○ The ones you've thought about
- ○ Ideas from your manager
- Feedback (mutual)

Don't feel comfortable with your manager? Talk to someone you trust and admire.

Once you feel your plan is solid, keep track of your progress!

One way of doing it is to keep track of your accomplishments MONTHLY. What do I mean by accomplishments?

I mean that my boss, and yours too, knows (or should know) what my main responsibilities are. What that person needs to know is how you made the work better.

For example:
From: Reviewed and analyzed various performance indicators, system statistics, and variances to identify trends, which are used for planning purposes and establishing preventive controls as needed.

To: Reduced budget variances by 12% and system downtimes by 32% through the design and utilization of control metrics. This led to robust estimates and increased planning accuracy.

Whoa! That girl is the bomb and I need her on my team like yesterday! Oh wait, that was me.

I kid you not, I had a reminder on my calendar every two weeks to write down my accomplishments. I also recommended that my team do something similar. That way, during your performance review period you can pick and choose the coolest things on your list, rather than waiting for your boss to notice, remember, or call out what you did. Believe me, the best way to get noticed by your boss is by making that person's life easier.

You also need a sounding board. Someone who you can bounce ideas off of and will challenge you to become a better person. Your manager may be this person. I have had great managers, okay managers, and pretty bad ones. I have been very blessed and when I had a great manager, that person was truly amazing.

In your case, start recruiting for a mentor, a coach, and a sponsor. But first, make sure you understand the differences between these roles.

The Coach
A coach helps you identify opportunities for improvement and growth, guides you to create a plan that works for you, and holds you accountable. It sounds something like this: "Last time we talked, you were excited about the upcoming interview for the new role, but today I hear you feeling a bit hesitant. What is bothering you?" "Can you think about a time when you were hesitant about starting something new and it turned out well? What did you learn from that?"

Your reaction might be: "Oh boy, I have to have the action plan my coach asked for ready before my next meeting."

The Mentor
A mentor provides subject-specific guidance based on anecdotes and brings perspective so you can keep your eye on the ball. It sounds like this: "When I was in your role, it was an implicit rule that you had a relationship with your peers in other lines of business. Is that on your

radar?" It also may sound like this: "When I used to run your department a while ago, our approval process for new system implementation had four steps. Is that still the case?"

Your reaction might be: "Hmm, I hadn't considered that before."

The Sponsor
A sponsor is your personal advocate, many times without you even knowing about it. It sounds like this: "Just FYI, the folks on the 30th floor were tossing around ideas about this transformational project that will cure all world diseases and I put your name out these."

Your reaction might be: "OMG. What have you done?"

That being said, I've armed myself with a complete board of directors. I've always believed in having a board of directors rather than one mentor or one coach. You see, a mentor is (typically) subject specific. Since I had multiple projects going at once that impacted multiple areas, I had to have more than one mentor. Also, I've always moved at 100 MPH, and people like me that have a certain amount of excessive focus (or as I call it, "insane achievement syndrome") grow out of our mentors quickly. Plus, the mentor and/or coach relationship is a mutual commitment that can take a lot of time on both ends. In my case, I preferred to dilute the responsibility of keeping me sharp.

This diagram demonstrates the board of directors concept.

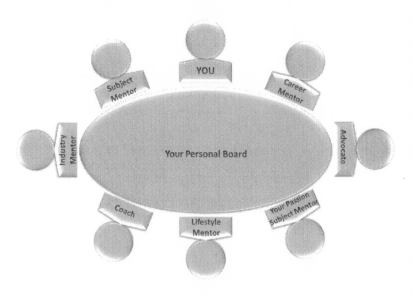

How do you fill those seats? **NETWORK**!

"**Each one of us**
must take responsibility
for our own lives, and above all, show
respect and love for living things
around us, specially each other."

~DR. JANE GOODALL

Chapter 3: Network

You would not think so with the number of connections I have, but can I tell you that I find networking terribly awkward?

The key has been to find something that works for me and exploit the heck out of that avenue. Like anything else, you are good at what you are good at, and the path to achieving your ultimate goals might be different than everyone else's.

For me, as an introvert at heart, social media and 1:1 meeting have proven to work best.

Early in my career, I initiated my networking journey within the four walls of my organization.

How did I get started? I began with the output from the exercises described in the previous chapters.

As I mentioned, I was always volunteering for this assignment or that project and although initially, I was not too structured about this approach to volunteering later on, I started to incorporate boundaries to align those volunteer initiatives with my professional goals. I still volunteered, but only as long as it sounded like a good opportunity for me to develop a specific skillset. This allowed me to observe numerous individuals firsthand. Some taught me the things that I would never do when I got to that level, and others were a reflection of specific characteristics that I wanted to emulate.

In the beginning, I would even volunteer to take notes for someone during a meeting. Although I recognize the danger in volunteering for the note taker role, especially for women, at that time it granted me access to the room while allowing me to be attentive and observant of the behaviors and interaction mechanics. I would observe and record those characteristics that resonated with my personal belief system. Later on, I would volunteer to run a section of the project, until I finally started to get my own projects.

Throughout all that volunteering, I was specifically attentive to folks that exhibited behaviors that I wanted to model. It did not matter who or whether they were women, men, cats, dogs, orange, or green. If they did something admirable, as subtle as it was, they were part of my list of people with great capabilities. These people became my targets. I just needed to understand their stories and (hopefully) the journey that eventually resulted in developing the skillset I admired. What did I do with my target list? I did the unthinkable: I reached out!

One by one, I reached out to them for a quick moment of their time. I must say that the first few times, I was petrified. I sheepishly talked (or typed when I reached out through email) while fighting with my internal voices. "Why the heck would he/she answer?" "Who do you think you are reaching out to the head of such-and-such?" "Just delete that email. It is not worth it. OMG, if your boss finds out, he/she will freak out that you are being a pest."

As time passed, I got better at the outreach. Additionally, I discovered that there was nothing to be worried about. People are generally willing to help, as long as:

- You bring your "A" game with you
- You are concise and targeted in your message
- You respect their time

Are there people who are not willing to help? Of course! Those who are not willing to help are typically silent, signaling me to move on.

As I write this, I must share that I just got blocked by the CEO of a company that I reached out to, after I ran into him at the supermarket earlier this week and made some small talk. It happens, but I promise it will not be the norm.

A few examples of my interactions:

- Interaction 1:
  - My role: Note taker
  - His role: Project manager
  - Outreach method: Company IM tool

- "Hi, while taking notes for project Magnolia, I realized that John was reporting results that were contradictory to the agreed plan. You respectfully called it out during the project, but I would like to understand the background that led to the established plan. Not sure if you have time to eat with everything on your plate, but can we chat over lunch?"

- Interaction 2:
  - My role: Team representative for Business Unit project
  - Her role: Executive sponsor
  - Outreach method: Cafeteria stalking (I have no shame about this).
  - "Hi, you probably don't know me but, I am the business unit lead for project Olympus. During our meeting last Tuesday, I noticed a few things that I would like to clarify before I bring them to the attention of my business unit. Would it be okay if we chat for a bit?"
    (I made sure to have a true shortlist by the time we met)

- Interaction 3:
  - My role: Program manager
  - His role: Head of the legal team
  - Outreach method: Program legal review meeting
  - "Wow, you opened my eyes to this legal risk that was right in front of us. Thanks for sharing. I need a mentor to learn more about the legal risks of my current and future initiatives. Would you mind if we caught up monthly? We can combine it with our program legal review meeting to save you time, and I would be delighted to return the favor for the upcoming new hires on your team."

- Interaction 4:
  - My role: Program manager for an enterprise-wide technology initiative
  - Her role: Company's new technology C-level executive
  - Outreach method: Cafeteria stalking. (Seriously. Humans get hungry and early in the morning, they are fresh and full of hope for the day... most of the time.)

- Initial interaction: "Hi, we met last night at project Frozen Mountain's launch party. Welcome to our company, you will love it here! I loved the part of your speech where you talked about women in technology. As a woman in technology myself, I would love to learn more about your journey. Can I treat you to coffee?
- During coffee (blown away by her nonchalant approach to challenges and her relatable journey): "This may sound different, but I never believed in having a single mentor relationship. I believe in having a personal board of directors to bounce ideas off of and gather different perspectives on my approach. Would you mind if I consider you part of my personal board and we had coffee quarterly?"
- Answer: "Absolutely. I 'll be part of your board!"
- "Wonderful. I'm not sure how I can return the favor yet, but I am sure we can figure it out together."

As you can see, there is nothing scary about reaching out, as long as you do your homework, strategize, and identify an intersection point. I am sure you prepare before giving a presentation or before giving a report on something you are working on. Networking with key individuals should be no different. Do your homework!

For me, I do not get out there without having these steps completed:

Target - Benchmark - Strategize - Plan - Execute

How about networking outside your own company? Uh, SCARY!

I must admit that this is my Achilles' heel, but I've also gotten slightly better as time goes on. That being said, to this day, every time I attend a large-scale event, especially at the very beginning, I suffer from what I call my 10 minutes of suck. It is not fear necessarily; it is more like huge discomfort about the potential of meaningless and forced conversations. I'm an introvert, remember? This does not deter me though. I force myself to attend at least one event every week and be present and socially available to whoever approaches me because I now realize that they may be feeling exactly the same way as me. In my case, I would rather climb through the walls, preferably unnoticed, go to my bed, crawl under the blankets, and read a good book. On the other hand, I realize how important networking is, so in spite of all the tantrums and drama inside my brain, I still go, still open up, and end up having a nice time with a series of strangers. Some of them are daring enough to give me their business contact information. Later on, I follow up.

You might think, well, I do not really have a business, so I do not have a need to network outside my company, or my favorite excuse: "But I am so busy already. I do not have time to network." Let me tell you that if you really want to grow professionally, explore what is happening outside the walls of your company, and see what new elements you can add to your work approach, you need to network. You do not need to go to every networking event. Just make sure you strategically pick events that align with your goals and growth strategy.

What other value might you get from the right networking events? Try these:

- Explore new job opportunities
- Discover new potential mentors or members of your personal board
- Learn how others address challenging situations
- Discover emerging trends
- Discover volunteering opportunities
- Showcase your wow factor
- Showcase your company's offerings
- Learn about new competitors
- Discover services that you can personally benefit from

I kid you not, it was during a networking event that I discovered one of those awesome fashion box companies that deliver several outfit options right to my doorstep. At another event, I was educated about the fact that people rent clothes instead of purchasing them for special events. Then another time I discovered that you can use gel nail polish for your toes. Who knew?

I have even more professional anecdotes, like finding my third employee while networking at a co-working space open house, and when a handshake quickly became an interview, followed by an offer the next morning. But the amusing stories make it more fun and at the end of the day, I am trying to convince you to get out there.

Like any meaningful experience, good networking takes time, effort, practice, and if you are like me, a non-natural networker, it takes strategizing and preparation. In my case, it takes LOTS of preparation because of my introverted nature that leads to needing lots and lots of personal space. Today's networking arena spans a lot of areas: social networking, professional networking, charity networking, community networking, and many more. You can have it all and for each of them, you need to rise to the occasion and prepare accordingly. As this is a professional development guidance book, I will focus on professional networking, and you probably guessed right: there are a lot of those too.

If you think about it, by having a clear purpose and your core values defined, you can navigate these events like a pro. With the output of the previous two chapters, make it a point to determine what your main motivators are, what you are trying to accomplish, what skills you are trying to develop, and what areas you have mastered. The output of this small exercise should give you a basic framework to determine the specific outcomes that would result in a successful networking event for you. This framework will enable you to step out of the small talk and meaningless conversations and go for deep conversations that enable you to connect with people.

Let me give you an example of pulling everything together:

Although I am an introvert, I need to work with people to thrive. I just need some quiet time after a while to fill up my jar.

Purpose: I've discovered (through A LOT OF WORK, coaching, and introspection) that my purpose is to feel spiritually connected, become a better version of myself, and inspire those around me to do the same.
Goal: My personal goal is to grow my business, which focuses on working with senior leaders to enhance the operational health of medium-sized organizations, enabling them to sustain growth and reduce operating cost, thus becoming a better version of themselves.

Activities: All my activities today, including volunteer activities, professional development, and engagements, support my purpose and goal.

Based on this, I go to networking events seeking these key elements:

- Discover opportunities where I can help and also learn from individuals on a similar journey to mine
- Find professionals that I can help or be helped by
- Find opportunities to connect like-minded professionals to available opportunities, therefore enhancing my credibility as a personal development advocate
- Rekindle previous professional relationships
- Find businesses that can use my help

And this last point is very important. When you are new to a networking group, especially when the organization hosting the event has been hosting them for a while and everyone else seems to know each other, you need to go with the mindset of "how can you help" first, rather than "how can they help". What you can gain (at least initially) should be a relationship. Over time, you will gain a lot, believe me, but you have to build up to that point, and that building takes time.

Are you thinking that you don't have anything to offer yet? Think again!

If you have completed the exercises in the first two chapters, you can guide someone through them. You may be a social media guru and can teach someone how to take care of their own social media accounts, or you can provide guidance to non-gurus on how to maximize their targets.

True story: I had one young woman in her junior year of college, God bless her, arrive to a jam-packed networking event with resume in hand and break in to a conversation that I was having with other senior professionals to say: "I am a communications major looking for an internship, but more than anything I want to learn about the consulting industry. For that reason, I was wondering if I could manage your social media accounts for free, and in that way, I can learn about the topics that are important in the industry and what people react to." I was stunned. I wanted to hire her as my life coach instead.

I can appreciate how difficult it is to meet new people in a new setting. Should you not have the drive of the above woman (I sure don't have it), you can use my favorite approach.

My top strategy is to start by searching the room for individuals that are still trying to scout their team or acquaintances. There is always someone that you can relate to because they look as uncomfortable as you. That should be your initial target. Once you establish an initial conversation, you scout for the next target.

Another strategy is to locate yourself close to the coffee. That way you can make eye contact with the first coffee taker and introduce yourself.

A few tips:

1. Be honest – it is fine to say "This is my first networking event".
2. Be yourself – I have started conversations with "Isn't networking awkward?"

3. Listen – before you sell anything, or anyone, listen. The other person always needs something. If you start by discovering that, you build your own credibility.

Once you go through the event and exchange business cards, write a little note on the back of the card, something that helps you remember that person. Do this as quickly as you can, preferably the same evening while in the car (not driving). Believe me, you will appreciate this the next day when everything starts to blend together and becomes a blur.

Some of my notes include the following:
- "The lady that just moved to our city and can't find good ethnic food."
- "The guy that has four kids in travel hockey."
- "Catherine's first boss when they worked at 123 Supply."
- "The lady with the fabulous shoes."
- "The eloquent young guy with the fabulous purple tie he got custom made."

How does this help? For one, it helps me tie the face to the name. Additionally, it helps me interject a personal note should I decide to email or call them to follow up and request time. I do follow up with everyone. EVERYONE! The reason is that you never know what synergies might come up or how we can help each other with current or future goals. Of course, I prioritize in-person chats based on my target goals and schedule some time to check in periodically, but overall, I do connect with everyone, and so should you.

Let's recap with some **parting thoughts.**

Networking is not collecting contacts. Networking is about planting relations.

~MISHA.AT

Chapter 4: Parting Thoughts

It is important to note that professional development and personal growth is neither a destination nor a particular goal to achieve, but rather it is a journey. As such, and like any other journey, it requires the vision of an endpoint to make the appropriate preparations.

Not sure where to go? Then ask questions of the people you meet and carefully listen to those answers. You can listen to podcasts, read biographies, and read professional blogs. Your destination might change, but if you do not start somewhere, it will be challenging to get anywhere.

Like the saying goes: If you don't know where you're going, any road will take you there.

I am a strong believer that complacency is the seed of stagnation, and stagnation is the root of unhappiness, eventually causing a million other problems. My advice? Get started with the exercises described throughout this book. Do not overanalyze the content you write; you can always go back and update as many times as you need.

Are you wondering what to do after getting to this point in this book? Well, for one, you celebrate because you have initiated a wonderful journey of self-empowerment and growth. As important as it is to dedicate effort and focus on your craft, it is also important to celebrate yourself as you accomplish small goals along the way. I had a boss that frequently said: "You do not need to eat the whole apple. Just take one bite at a time." That saying sums up the best way to achieve your biggest goals: Take it one day at a time. Do you have a big goal? Break it down into small increments and celebrate each of those milestones. This will motivate you, and this motivation is extremely necessary, along with self-discipline, so that you can achieve your milestones and continue to progress through your journey.

Following that celebratory moment, start again from the beginning. This book should serve as a guide that you can use any time you feel you have reached a professional plateau and are ready for the next step. The good news is that you do not have to start from scratch, but rather adjust your goals and your self-assessment exercise. New professional goal? Revisit the path, course correct as necessary, and execute.

As you move through your journey, it is always important to keep a few things in mind:

Professional development and growth are hard work, but they become manageable when you surround yourself with the right people.
Like any long journey, part of your support should be to surround yourself with amazing people. You have no idea how many individuals I had to fire from my personal board, or from my circle of "close friends". Yes, that includes creating some distance from some family members and certain "close" friends. Today, I am VERY at peace with those decisions. I had enough challenges to overcome and could not afford to add the challenges

brought by negative thoughts, criticism, or fear-based thoughts from others.

Do not get me wrong, EVERYONE has good days and bad days, but you need to pay attention to the outcome of the majority of the interactions. The people that consistently question your journey to success and challenge you with judgment disguised as either jokes or "concerns" do not belong in your inner circle. There should be no guilt on your part either. You have to remember that everyone has their own goals and their own journeys to follow. As you respect their journeys, you should demand them to respect yours. Additionally, those around you may be battling their own personal limitations and challenges. As caring as their comments may be, they have nothing to do with you, and that is how it should stay. You always have the option of establishing boundaries with the individuals that do not fill your soul. The reality of it is that you are the average of the handful of people you surround yourself with. I'm not sure about you, but I have as high expectations for me as I do for the people that surround me. In short: YOU HAVE TO FIND YOUR TRIBE!

Now, I do not mean that you should only surround yourself with people that tell you how pretty you are when you have toothpaste on your shirt and have not combed your hair in a few days. What I mean is that you should surround yourself with people that, through constructive feedback, encouragement, support, and their own examples, enable you to achieve your goals.

This applies to the individuals you help as well as the individuals that help you. I've had many mentees over the years, some of them have been exceptional, but one thing I am firm about is steering away from defeat because that mentality spreads. I am the first cheerleader for each of my peeps, the first one to explore potential new ways of addressing challenges. I coach them to explore and tap into their undiscovered potential and brainstorm ways in which they can re-strategize their approach. Knowing that there will be bad days, I am the first one to give a helping hand where needed. However, I can't take a consistent mindset of defeat and victimhood. I will help you get out, but I do need to see a desire to get out.

As you navigate towards your target individuals and try to align yourself to form key partnerships, make sure that you do a bit of homework on those individuals before reaching out. What do they care about? What is their background? What causes do they support? Why? For one, these can become great conversation starters and enable you to avoid the dreaded small talk. Second, it gives you the necessary basics to identify intersections with your interests, and more importantly, areas in which you can provide value.

Professional development and growth should be a holistic approach to addressing your overall brand. The way that you portray yourself dictates the pace of your growth. Everyone is busy. Everyone is **VERY** busy, and the leaders within an organization will not take the time to elevate your capabilities, mentor you, or coach you if their efforts are not going to be taken seriously. Think about it for a second. Let's say that you decide to volunteer. Would you continue to volunteer if your efforts were never appreciated? If every single time you were received with a cold shoulder? Sure, there are going to be times where people are not in a good place emotionally, but that should be the exception and not the norm of your interactions. In the same way, it is going to be difficult for a mentor to periodically carve out time for you if that time is not being appreciated.

Before you reach out to someone, do a little self-evaluation for a minute. Some questions that might help are the following:
- How might my message be interpreted?
- How is my presence coming across?
- How are my actions impacting those around me?

Self-awareness is an invaluable characteristic of the best leaders I've known. As human beings, we think that what we do and how we do it is the best way, but is it really?

Another element to consider when thinking about the way that your persona comes across is that, whether we like it or not, ALL of us have implicit biases that facilitate some of our daily decision-making process. Biases are pre-assumed conceptions we form to expedite decision making. The good news is that a lot us are working on being intentional and diminishing the instances of unfairly pre-judging. The bad news is that we are not always going to get it right because we are human. One way to overcome this is to prepare yourself and bring your "A" game at all times.

Confidence, assertive answers (even when the answer is "I don't know") and a polished presence are always great kick starters to help the recipient be open to interacting with you. Think about the times when you have been quiet during meetings, or the times when you have been way too shy during a networking event. While you may have been petrified to say a word, the person close to you perceived you as uninterested or bothered. You never know who is watching and when your opportunity is going to show up, so it's better to always be prepared and bring your best self.

It is also important for you to consider whether you are showing up in person or on social media. Remember that the way you find people, learn about their interests, and identify synergies for collaboration is the same way they use to find you and learn about your interests.

Let that sink in for a minute before moving on.

Professional development and growth are not a sprint, but more of a marathon.

I am a strong believer that failure offers the best platform for future success. You see, if you have a positive mindset, failure strips down perceptions and "hard set" beliefs, allowing you to climb through the window of limitless possibilities. As you prepare for your development and growth marathon, expect to fail often and to be disappointed. Then learn to dust yourself off and keep going equally as often.

There is a huge difference between tripping over and falling vs. being unable to stand back up. In your journey, there is also a big difference between being disappointed for a bit and defeated with a victim mentality. Learn to recognize the two when they appear in your journey. Notice that I said "when" and not "if". They will happen, so you might as well prepare for it with a plan B, and sometimes a plan C too. The other day I read a quote that said: "Success is not final, failure is not fatal. It is the courage to continue that counts."

You might be thinking: "But you are saying I should do this, and evaluate that, and I already have a full-time job, 15 kids, and 3 dogs. How will I take care of elevating my career as well?" Well, I am about to add something else. As part of running your marathon or a series of marathons, you also need to prioritize self-care. You need to remember that when you do not take care of yourself you can't take care of others. When you are not well, you can't do anything else, as you will be giving scraps to those you take care of. Every marathon runner I know fuels their bodies with efficient foods. Competitive marathoners add supplements, therapy, training, and coaches. The harder the race, the more preparation, and fuel it requires. It is up to you how you handle your self-care, but at the bare minimum, you need time to fill up your cup, through the method that best elevates your spirit.

Arianna Huffington says: "We take good care of our phones, plugging them in everywhere there is an outlet. We should be at least half as diligent with ourselves."

When? Let me give you an example. You remember that time when you had a paper due in college and someone invited you to happy hour? And you went, and had fun even though you did not have a drink because you had that paper to complete? That is how you do it. You make time.

Maybe you take an afternoon off to work on your self-assessment and turn off the data plan of your phone to avoid social media distractions. Maybe you wake up a little earlier for a couple of days. Maybe you skip Netflix for two weeks straight, or maybe instead of having lunch outside, you take your lunch to a nearby conference room and lock the door.

Additionally, with technology at our fingertips, you can listen to a podcast while cooking, or put an audiobook on while you are commuting to or from work.

The possibilities are endless when you get creative.

And finally...

Professional development and growth are sweeter when you share them with others.

You have worked, you have developed, you have grown. Now what?

Share your knowledge and help others rise!

If you are a manager, your top responsibility is to influence and help your team accomplish your organization's goals. The best way to gain credibility and trust is to change your focus from control to influence and support. This can be accomplished through honesty, vulnerability, and by having a vested interest in helping each of the individuals on your team elevate their skills and capabilities to new levels. I attended a marketing seminar recently where the presenter opened by stating, "I am no expert on the topic, but I want to share what I've learned thus far." I have never seen a more attentive class throughout the whole two-hour duration.

It is difficult to be a great manager if you have not had a great manager yourself. However, at this point, you have risen to the challenge and proved that it can be accomplished. Now there are people under you looking at how you present yourself and how you operate. Once you are invested in your growth plan, and preferably when you have at least one or two goals under your belt, make sure that you take care of your peeps and help them rise as you climb. You owe it to yourself to keep climbing and to those that are behind you to show them the way.

If you are not a manager yet, think about ways in which you can help more junior rising stars and get them started on their own journeys. You can volunteer your time in a structured way or in a less formal way with your coworkers. The easiest way to begin a structured volunteering program is through the school you attended in the past by serving as a mentor to students. Other less formal options are to volunteer to mentor the interns that come during the summer, or maybe your company's new hires. Want to step away from a direct connection to your company? You can volunteer with an organization tied to your personal passions, where you can challenge yourself and use your developed skills in a different environment, which will allow you to continue to grow. These days, there are numerous organizations dedicated to serving the community that surrounds you in countless ways. Explore your surroundings, ask your network, and align yourself with the one that speaks most closely to your personal mission and passions.

Is your schedule crazy? Then how about writing or recording a blog post, or maybe writing an article where you share your growth path? The path you went through and the challenges you overcame can become a tool for the success of others experiencing similar challenges as you did. Remember that in all cases, what you do for others for the benefit of your surroundings ultimately comes back to help you.

So, after finding your purpose, relentlessly striving to become your best self, and arming yourself with the best alliances, what can stop you?

I say nothing!

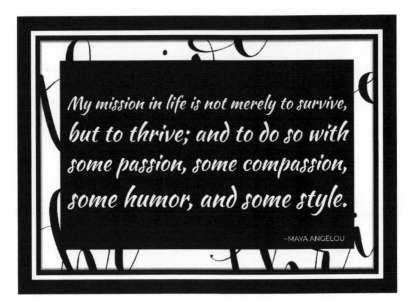

My mission in life is not merely to survive, but to thrive; and to do so with some passion, some compassion, some humor, and some style.

~MAYA ANGELOU

Acknowledgements

There are several people that I am grateful to for serving as the lever that throws me into the next step once I have reached the current goal. They all keep me going towards excellence: Dr. Cristina Gonzalez, Migdalia Rodriguez, Audrey Russo, Kelly Fetick, Shannon Gregg, John Miller, and my departed friend Elisabet Rodriguez. Thanks for being **TRUE** advocates, cheerleaders, and friends.

To my mom for being the voice of practical reason and calming guidance.

To my daughters Natalia and Ana Sofia, thank you for your patience, your encouraging words, and specially for your independence. Your interesting marketing suggestions sure made mami think innovatively...most definitely outside the box where there was no box, to begin with.

Above and beyond all these key people, I would be a huge pile of yarn if it wasn't for my supportive and encouraging husband Miguel Gonzalez, Jr. Thanks for actively pushing me to become a better version of myself and for nodding and holding in your scared face with my crazy ideas. I could not have chosen a better partner for this speed race.